Into the Storm

Debi Adams

CONTENTS

Special Thanks

Acknowledgements

Introduction

Special thanks!

I would like to give thanks first of all to God for it is by Him and through Him that I can accomplish anything. I also want to thank my wonderful husband for all of his love and support. He has always seen me for who I would become and not for who I was. Without his patience and love this book would have never been written.

The writing of this work would not have been possible without the permission of Rev. William Claire Greiner. It was his publication about eagles on the internet that inspired me to write this book. The research for the eagles comes primarily from him. Although I have never met this man, he gave me permission via email to use his work in any way that would bring honor to God. So it is with great appreciation of his work of eagles that I present my story. My prayer is that you will be as blessed by his work as I was, and that you learn to rise above your storms.

I also want to thank Bob & Debbie Santos, Frank Basaggio, Duane Adams, Elaine Green, Mary Lou Friedline, Debbie Dillard, Kevin Simpson, Pati Livengood, and the intercessors at LifeSpring Christian Church. Whether you realize it or not, you have all played a part in my journey of writing this book.

Finally, I want to express my gratitude to my mother-in-law, Joy Adams, for introducing my husband to God at an early age. Her love and devotion to "Daddy God" has always been a wonderful example to follow.

Acknowledgements

God has sent me many angels in human form along the way. This is how I refer to the people God sent me to encourage me to finish this book. Although this book is not very long it took many people along the way to cause me to bring this book to completion. God brought a wonderful woman of God into our church for a brief time to encourage me. Dee Marker was one of my angels in human form. She and her husband Barrie now live out of state. The very first time we met, she began to prophecy that I needed to finish what God has given me. She never even knew about the book. Every time I called her she encouraged me to finish the book.

I was also sent an encourager by the name of John Christman. He was the person that God used to take us to see our very first eagles nest. Dale would take me to one of the state parks here in Pennsylvania to eagle watch whenever I needed encouraged. It is three hours away from our home and they have eight pair of eagles there but they are in a protected area and you need strong binoculars to watch them. We went one holiday just to see these majestic birds. When we were about to leave that day a gentleman approached us and asked if we were eagle watching. My husband explained that we were watching them, but we were not having much success that day. He offered to take us to a special place of his where he and his dog had found an eagle's nest. We were so excited! When we got there we could hardly believe our eyes. The mother eagle was feeding two eaglets in the nest.

Introduction

Long before I knew why God had put it in my heart, "On Eagle's Wings," was my favorite song. The lyrics of the song would become the cry of my heart: "Here I am waiting, Abide in me, I pray, Here I am longing for you, Hide me in your arms… Come breathe in me, and I will rise on eagle's wings."

Since a child often believes what she has been told, I spent most of my youth feeling worthless. I never understood why my grandmother tore me down. She lived with us from the time I was three years old until she passed away when I was sixteen. I used to cry myself to sleep, often regretting being born. My childhood placed in me an overwhelming lack of confidence.

It has taken me many years to overcome the verbal abuse I endured as a child. But it has been the discovery of God's great love that set me on an incredible journey of healing. God was so interested in bringing me to a place of healing that He used the flight of an eagle to get my attention. This book is a result of my journey with God to mount up on wings of eagles above the storms in my life. It is my prayer that you too will overcome the storms in your life and experience healing.

Chapter 1

Storms

Then the Lord answered Job out of the storm. Job 38:1 NIV

It is very important to understand that storms are a necessary part of life.

I never understood the importance of storms until God began speaking to me about the life of the eagle. I have always wanted my life to be free from anything disturbing. Maybe it was this way because I have encountered several storms in my life. My husband's favorite scripture is found in Psalm 139:15-16. It states that *"all of our days are written in a book before one of them came to be,"* even the storms of our lives. So I wish to share the story of my life with you so that you can experience rising above the difficulties in your life.

One of the books God placed in my hands is a book by: Holly Wagner called, "When it Pours He Reigns." It is an excellent book about overcoming life's storms. In this book she revealed that in 1991 an artificial environment called Biosphere 2 was created in Oracle, Arizona. The scientist found that after two years a number of trees became weak and bent over. Some even broke. They had simulated almost all of the elements of weather they could imagine......except the wind. The scientists discovered that without the stress of wind, the trees were weak. They had the perfect soil, the perfect amount of water and sun, and they grew... but they never faced a storm.

It is the storms in our lives that build our strength. This is also seen in the life of the eagle. Researchers have found if you assist an eaglet in the process of breaking out of the egg the eaglet will die. It is in the struggle that the eaglet becomes strong. The storms in our lives are not meant to destroy us, but to give us the strength we will need to survive the rest of the journey.

The Love of God is so amazing! God loved us first and He continues to love us regardless of what we do. God longs to take the brokenness in our lives and "give us beauty for ashes, the oil of joy for mourning, and the garment of praise for the spirit of heaviness." (Isa. 61:3) You see, Jesus died on the cross so we might have life. The cross is a place of divine exchange. I used to think I was of no use due to the brokenness of my life.

How wrong I was! We are the vessels God chooses to use. It was also the revelation that scars are a proof of healing that gave me the true picture of the power of Christ. You see God uses broken things. It was the broken alabaster box that released the anointing! The alabaster box represents that which contains the anointing oil or Spikenard. As Christians, we are the vessels that contain Christ, "The Anointed One."

It is wonderful that out of everywhere in the universe that Christ could dwell, He chose to live in us! So we are the bottle, the vessel, the alabaster box, that contains the oil of the Holy Spirit, or the presence of God. The oil represents the anointing. We need to see that it was not only the oil (which is Christ the Anointed One) that was of great worth, but also the vessel that contained the oil. We seldom realize our value in Christ! Everyone questioned the sinful woman, because she used up a whole years wages in the cost of anointment she poured on Christ, we often question our value not remembering the price Jesus paid for us. As Vance Havner wrote in the Christian Reader, Volume 32, No. 4, "it is the broken soil that produces a crop, the broken clouds that give rain, broken grain gives bread and it is broken bread that gives strength." It was Peter, weeping bitterly, who returned to greater power. It was the broken body of Christ that purchased your salvation. You exchange your brokenness for wholeness, your sadness for joy, your ashes for beauty, and your failures for His victory! The list goes on and on. I hope by the end of this book you will look at your life differently and see your storms as agents to position you closer to the God that emptied heaven for you.

Have you ever seen the movie "Twister," where the characters chase tornados? They track the storm, so they can learn from it. I've never considered myself a storm watcher, but I have been in enough of them to know that we need to learn the lessons God has given us in the life of the eagle. By their examples we will not only learn to face the difficulties in our life, but we will learn to rise above them.

My husband and I were on vacation once when a hurricane watch was issued. We prayed about what to do and had a peace to stay and face the storm.

As we watched many people in our hotel leave we spoke with the hotel manager. He told us he had seen many hurricanes over the years. What we experienced was amazing! We watched the storm come and go. But the most interesting part of the storm was when the eye of the storm went through.

The winds and waves were the worst I had ever seen. But when the eye of the storm went through there was a complete calm. Everything got totally quiet. There was perfect peace! I believe God is the eye of the storm. This would explain why everything returns to complete peace. After the eye of the storm passed, the weather was the most beautiful I had ever seen. I know God is in all the storms I face and that he has a perfect calm that will follow. He will work everything out for our good through the difficulties we face, if we look to him in the midst of it.

Eagles, by God's design, know how to use the power of the storm to lift them above it. Storms will always be a part of our life on this earth, so we need to learn how to rise above them. Matt 5:45 tells us that it rains on the just and the unjust. Everyone goes through storms. So let's learn the lesson from the storms that the eagle can teach us.

Chapter 2

Flight Training

"For physical training is of some value, but godliness has value for all things, holding promise for both the present life and the life to come." I Tim. 4:8 NIV

It is very important to learn how to fly before taking flight. Pilots have seen eagles at very high altitudes, but both pilots and eagles had to learn to fly before taking that kind of flight. We will learn how to soar by reading and applying God's word to our lives. There are 34 references of eagles throughout the bible. God must have thought the eagles were important enough to refer to them so many times.

I heard a saying once that a man never learns to be a good sailor on calm seas. It is in the raging sea that his sailing skills increase. The storms in our life are not meant to destroy us but to take us higher in God. They are intended to takes us to heights we could not reach without them. The storms are just instruments whose purposes arc to cause us to reach heavenly places. These heights could not be reached without the power they release. Oh, if you just get this revelation, you will never look at storms the same again. You see God rides upon the winds and the waves obey Him. God is always with you. The eagle knows the purpose of the storm! They are designed to cause us to rise higher in God, so we can soar high above everything that would keep us from the presence of God. The following is a list of things we need to know in order to take flight:

- God is in your storm.
- Look to Him and not at the storm.
- Believe that as you surrender your will, His will and purpose will come from the storm.
- Have confidence in the one who is writing your story.
- God is the author and finisher of your faith.
- He who has begun a good work in you will complete it.
- Allow the wind of the spirit to take you higher so you will have His perspective.
- Have peace in the midst of your storm by keeping your mind on Him.
- Enjoy the calm after the storm.

I am just learning to soar, and the few times I have experienced soaring with God have been amazing. The first time I experienced soaring was after a car wreck I had on my way home from a very difficult day at work. As I was driving home, I felt very upset and the feelings of being inadequate began to surface. It's amazing to me that the devil only uses our past against us and we still fall for it. Growing up, I felt so inadequate that I used to cry myself to sleep. Well this was one day when the past seemed to envelope me. I didn't recognize that it was an attack! So as I drove home, I was very sad. We need to be very careful who or what we agree with! You see, the Bible tells us that the place of agreement is the place of power. Don't let yourself agree with anything you think about yourself unless it lines up with who God says you are. The devil is not all knowing like God, and that's why he uses our past against us, because he knows our past. But as Christians our past has been washed clean by the forgiveness of God. I really like what Carmen says in one of his songs; "when the devil reminds you of your past, just remind him of his future." Speak the name of Jesus because this will cause the devil to flee.

This is what I should have done, but I didn't recognize a storm was approaching. A storm in the form of a car wreck that is. Storms take many forms. There are relationship storms, health storms, and financial storms, just to name a few. But on this particular day, my approaching storm was a car wreck! I was traveling on a very small, narrow, and curvy country road. As I approached one very bad curve, I took the turn too sharp. The sun was in my eyes and I did not see the car approaching. I was just across the center line enough to hit the car head on. This was my first car wreck, and I sure did not act like the Debi I know. The wreck was my fault. Nothing looked good, but in the midst of my storm I began to apply the lessons I'd learned from the eagles. I sat in the car and waited until I could sense God. I just began praying. Not only was I praying, but I had allowed the forces of the storm to lift me high enough to hear God's voice. God spoke to me in a very small voice, and said, "Trust me, everything is Father Filtered. "

As a child of God, everything has to go through my father before it gets to me. So if God allowed it, then God would work it out for good. As I began to trust God, I started to soar higher towards him. God then gave me the ability to force my car door open and get out and check on the drive of the car I hit. By the power of my awesome God she and her grandson were unharmed. I called the

13

police and just waited as God and I continued in sweet fellowship. I apologized to the woman and offered my assistance. When the police came, I took full responsibility.

Because I was truly trusting God from my heart, the policeman said anyone could have made the mistake I made and didn't find me at fault. When my husband arrived, he could not believe his eyes. I was calm, confident in God and not shaken at all by the wreck. This was so far out of character for me. I took flight for the first time in my life during this storm. I had an encounter with God like I have never experienced.

In the end, everything was taken care of by my insurance but the most important thing was that I took flight. We are going to begin flight training so please learn the following steps so you can learn to soar.

One of the first lessons the eagle teaches us is to wait. I have never been very good at waiting. But as I look at the life of the eagle, I can see the benefit it offers. There are things in life we will never possess if we are not willing to wait. Even Jesus had to wait until the fullness of time to go to the cross. The eagle can fly at anytime, but it chooses to wait until it can soar. If the air is absolutely still with no movement an eagle cannot soar.

While other birds are taking flight the eagle patiently waits for the sun's rays to warm the earth's air currents, which are needed for effortless flight. The eagle usually only spends about two minutes per hour flapping its wings! The rest of the time, it is soaring.

We need to wait on God's Son, Jesus Christ. As Christians, we become weary doing things in our own strength. Isaiah 40:28-31 teaches us that, "The Lord is the everlasting God, the Creator of the ends of the earth. He will not grow tired or weary, and His understanding no one can fathom. He gives strength to the weary, and increases the power of the weak. Even youth grow tired and weary, and young men stumble and fall, but those who wait upon the Lord will renew their strength. They will soar on wings like eagles."

It's very important to understand that the word "wait" in this portion of scripture means to: hope or expect. So, waiting on God is not just sitting doing nothing. While we wait, we need to hope and look eagerly for God and expect to receive from Him. Psalms 37: 7 tells us to *"Rest in the Lord and wait patiently for Him."* Eagles wait patiently for the moving of the wind. The Hebrew word for wind is "ruwach" (roo-akh), and means "breath. " It is the same word for "Spirit."

We should wait for the moving of God's Spirit. We should wait patiently and expectantly. What would be the outcome if you got what you expected? When God first began speaking to me about eagles, He asked me what I would have if He instantly gave me what I was expecting to receive from Him. I had to be truthful and answer, "Not much, Lord." It's very important that our expectations are rooted and grounded in God and in His word. We need to have good expectations, because we have a good God.

There was a time in my life when I did not know how to have good expectations. My inability to have good expectations was due to the fact that I did not know God personally as a good God. I could believe God to be good for everyone except me, because I believed that I did not deserve anything good. How easy is it to believe for other people, but we don't believe for ourselves. Sometimes this happens because we see God filtered through the image of our earthly father. The journey God took me on was a journey to discover truth. John 8:32 teaches us that *"the truth will set you free."* Forgiveness was the key to changing my expectations into God-centered truths. This was the beginning of expecting good things from God. I had to forgive my earthly father, grandmother, and sister for the hurts and disappointments they had caused in my life.

God taught me that you cannot give what you do not have. My father did not give me the acceptance that I needed because he never received it himself. I finally realized that the rejection that I had faced as a child was not my fault. My father was never accepted as a child, so he did not have what I wanted him to give me. I took the blame for everything when it was never about me!

One day God spoke to me in a modern day parable to give me a revelation that would set me free. He gave me a picture of asking my neighbor for a loaf of bread, just to find out they did not have any. In my disappointment I left upset that they had no bread to give me. God told me this is what I did with my father. I was upset with him for not giving me something he did not possess. This revelation set me free. The truth will always set you free. I forgave my father and released myself from a prison of unforgiveness. Release those you have put in a prison of unforgiveness and you will be set free as well.

When I forgave I could finally see my Heavenly Father as good. I now expect good because I have learned the power of forgiveness. In James 1:17 we learn that *"Every good and perfect gift is from above."* And God says in Jeremiah 32:40 *"I will never stop doing good for you."*

One of the most powerful and anointed letters I have ever read is a love letter from the heart of God. It is available by going to www.thefathersloveletter.com. The letter is taken from scriptures in the bible. A copy of the letter is listed below.

AN INTIMATE MESSAGE FROM GOD TO YOU.
My Child…

You may not know me, but I know everything about you.
Psalm 139:1
I know when you sit down and when you rise up.
Psalm 139:2
I am familiar with all your ways.
 Psalm 139:3
Even the very hairs on your head are numbered.
Matthew 10:29-31
For you were made in my image.
 Genesis 1:27
In me you live and move and have your being.
 Acts 17:28
For you are my offspring.
 Acts 17:28
I knew you even before you were conceived.
Jeremiah 1:4-5
I chose you when I planned creation.
Ephesians 1:11-12
You were not a mistake, for all your days are written in my book.
 Psalm 139:15-16

I determined the exact time of your birth and where you would live.
Acts 17:26
You are fearfully and wonderfully made.
 Psalm 139:14
I knit you together in your mother's womb.
 Psalm 139:13
And brought you forth on the day you were born.
 Ps. 71:6
I have been misrepresented by those who don't know me.
John 8:41-44
I am not distant and angry, but am the complete expression of love.
1 John 4:16
And it is my desire to lavish my love on you.
 1 John 3:1
Simply because you are my child and I am your Father.
I John 3:1
I offer you more than your earthly father ever could.
Matthew 7:11
 I am the perfect father.
Matthew 5:48
Every good gift that you receive comes from my hand.
James 1:17
For I am your provider and I meet all your needs.
 Matthew 6:31-33
My plan for your future has always been filled with hope.
Jeremiah 29:11
Because I love you with an everlasting love
 Jeremiah 31:3
My thoughts toward you are countless as the sand on the seashore
 Psalms 139:17-18

And I rejoice over you with singing.
Zephaniah 3:17
I will never stop doing good to you.
Jeremiah 32:40
For you are my treasured possessions.
Exodus 19:5
I desire to establish you with all my heart and all my soul.
Jeremiah 32:41
And I want to show you great and marvelous things.
Jeremiah 33:3
If you seek me with all your heart, you will find me.
Deuteronomy 4:29
Delight in me and I will give you the desires of your heart.
Psalm 37:4
For it is I who gave you those desires
 Philippians 2:13
I am able to do more for you than you could possibly imagine.
Ephesians 3:20
For I am your greatest encourager
2 Thessalonians 2:16-17
I am also the Father who comforts you in all your troubles.
2 Corinthians 1:3-4
When you are brokenhearted, I am close to you.
Psalms 34:18
As a shepherd carries a lamb, I have carried you close to my heart.
 Isaiah 40:11
One day I will wipe away every tear from your eyes.
Revelation 21:3-4
And I'll take away all the pain you have suffered on this earth.
 Revelation 21:3-4

I am your Father, and I love you even as I love my son, Jesus.
John 17:23

For in Jesus, my love for you is revealed.
John 17:26

He is the exact representation of my being.
Hebrews 1:3

He came to demonstrate that I am for you, not against you.
Romans 8:31

And to tell you that I am not counting your sins.
2 Corinthians 5:18-19

Jesus died so that you and I could be reconciled.
2 Corinthians 5:18-19

His death was the ultimate expression of my love for you.
1 John 4:10

I gave up everything I loved that I might gain your love.
Romans 8:31-32

If you receive the gift of my son Jesus, you receive me.
1 John 2:23

And nothing will ever separate you from my love again.
Romans 8:38-39

Come home and I'll throw the biggest party heaven has ever seen.
Luke 15:7

I have always been Father, and will always be Father.
Ephesians 3:14-15

My question is…Will you be my child?
John 1:12-13

I am waiting for you.
Luke 15:11-32

Love, Your Dad - Almighty God
* Words paraphrased from the Holy Bible ©1999-2008
FathersLoveLetter.com

Chapter 3

Rising Above the Storms

"because of the tender mercy of our God by which the rising sun will come to us from heaven. Luke 1:78 NIV

Let's look at the wisdom God has given the eagle! The eagles know when a storm is approaching long before it arrives. They will fly to a high place and wait for the winds to come. When the storm hits the eagle sets its wings so the wind will lift it above the storm. Psalms 31:20 tells us; *"in the shelter of your presence you hide them."* We need to find the place of safety in His presence.

I mentioned that in Psalm 139:15-16 God tells us that all of our days are written in a book before one of them began. I had to experience several storms in my life before I could truly understand the significance and power of this scripture. I knew this scripture but I did not live like I knew it. It is one thing to know the word of God, but it is empowering to live it.

I needed the storms that came in various forms to cause me to live this scripture. I have never really trusted that God was in control. Because I grew up in an environment that constantly reinforced my negative feelings about myself, it created in me an inability to really trust God. I had a very wrong concept of God. I knew that God was good, and felt that I could believe in and trust Him for other people's needs. But I did not feel worthy enough to receive for myself what I could ask Him to do for others.

Due to the storms in my life, I am finally beginning to live what I believe. I used to feel if God did not intervene in my affairs in a positive way, then it was because I deserved it. I really never liked myself very much. How sad this is to admit, but the truth has set me free!

Freedom began when I learned how to forgive myself. It had always been easier for me to forgive others. God was requiring me to forgive myself, one day I tried to explain that I just couldn't do what He was asking. The Lord spoke to me and said, "Well, Deb, I guess the cross was not good enough for you." I was shocked by the very thought of this statement, and then I realized that by not forgiving myself, this was what I was proclaiming. I was telling God that His shed blood was good enough to forgive everyone and everything except me. It was this realization that set me free to forgive myself. The love of God is so powerful; it penetrated the years of wrong thinking that I had established.

The process of securing a job to assist my husband in the ministry has been one of the greatest storms of my life. God had to change my view of me, into His view of me. This process is still taking place. I am beginning to realize it has never been about me, my abilities or inabilities, but about His divine plan that I am becoming who He intended me to be.

I heard a story about an eagle that was raised in a chicken coop. By God's design this eaglet had been given the ability to fly higher than all birds and yet, this poor eagle surrounded by flightless birds never learned to fly. This is often what happens to us as Christians.

Due to the surroundings we have been placed in, we

look at the surrounding and not to the one who created us. I may have grown up in a chicken coop, but I am becoming the eagle I was meant to be.

God provided a perfect storm for me in the image of my first job in Pennsylvania. I became a secretary at a tool and die shop. It was an amazing miracle to me that I even got the job. But God was coming to me riding on a storm that I could not have imagined. I loved the job, but over the seven years I worked there I felt as if it was going to destroy me. I loved what I did, but I was not treated well at this job, which just reinforced how I felt about myself. This was a wrong image that my environment had built in me. After working at this job for seven years I finally got the courage to resign the position and look for another job. During the entire time I worked at this position I was constantly looking for another place of employment but God wanted me to take a leap of faith. It was not until I quit my job that God opened an amazing door for me as a secretary of a trucking company. By God's design, I would only be employed there for nine months before the company relocated to an area too far for me to travel. However, it was there at this place of employment that God blessed me more than words can tell.

God provided an atmosphere of people there that I will forever remember as my friends. This was an amazing place of acceptance, something the environment I grew up in never provided. I often said that rejection was my closet friend. As I was complaining to God one day about the rejection I had experienced in my life, I heard the Lord say, "If I walked a road of rejection for you, and you are to take up my cross and follow me, then you will walk a road of rejection too." Jesus walked a road of rejection by keeping His eyes on His Father, not on the storm of rejection that He found Himself in.

Jesus knew no matter what type of rejection He faced He would always have the love and acceptance of His Father. As Christians, we have the same Father and the same assurance of unending love and acceptance. The problem we have in this world is that we often view our Heavenly Father through the experiences of our earthly fathers. I had to learn that man's imperfections will never take away from the perfection of God. I also experienced the ability of my Heavenly Father to take the ashes in my life and make beauty out of them. This is one of the promises we have as His children. I know if you have ashes in your life but still no beauty, then God isn't finished with it yet.

God used a supervisor at the trucking company who became a father figure in my life to show me the acceptance that I lacked as a child. I am sure he has no idea that God used him in such a profound way to bring beauty to the ashes in my life. He did this in what may seem like a simple way to most people, but it healed a part of my broken heart. He collected die cast trucks and only had one very rare truck of the company we worked for, and on my last day of work he gave it to me. Due to the fact that he was old enough to be my father and I needed to experience value from a father, this did amazing things for me. My father was a wonderful man of God who, although he loved me, he did not possess the ability to show me the acceptance I needed, because as a child, he was not accepted. Someone cannot give you what he or she does not possess. After I left this job, God provided another job just in time for me to receive major surgery I had no idea was needed in my life. Why do we find it so difficult to trust for our current situations when God has cared so well for us in the past? When we can't see the hand of God in our current storm we need to trust that His heart for us is good.

Forgiveness is the key to blessing and is necessary if we want to rise above the storms in our lives. I had to learn that forgiveness is a choice. We cannot go by how we feel or what the circumstances around us tell us. We can not control what happens to us in life, but we get to choose our response to what happens to us. What is your response going to be?

Forgiveness = Victory
Unforgiveness = Defeat
Forgiveness = Soaring above the storms
Unforgiveness = Storm tossed

The road to healing all the hurts in your life is forgiveness. Choose the road of forgiveness.

Do you choose to be bitter or better because of the unjust things you have endured?

The word forgiveness means, "To untie a knot." I've heard it said, forgiveness is like unlocking the doors to a prison and letting someone free, just to discover the prisoner was you! You are the only one who holds the key to your prison. Just remember forgiveness is the key. Forgiveness and repentance are necessary if we are to be overcomers and rise above the storms in our lives.

I had the privilege of going to an aviary in Pittsburgh, Pennsylvania one day after church. The morning news had advertised they were having free admission. My husband knew how much it would mean for me to go see the eagles, so he changed his busy schedule to take me. It's hard to put into words how seeing these majestic birds affected me.

I knew God had created them to rise above the storms, so I wanted to learn from them. It really surprised me that the two eagles we saw were in an open area. They were behind a glass window that had no roof, only open sky. I asked the tour guide what kept them from flying away. She said if I would look at them very closely, I would see that both eagles were missing a wing. They had been injured and rescued. This is how they obtained the eagles. I discovered one eagle had been shot and the other had injured itself by flying into power lines.

God spoke a great revelation to me about their circumstances. One eagle could no longer soar because an enemy took one of its wings, and the other eagle lost its ability to soar due to its own error. This picture is true of us as Christians. Sometimes we allow others to keep us from soaring and other times it's our own choices that remove our wings. It's very comforting to discover that God has already provided a way of escape for us in both situations.

Isaiah 54:17 states that "No weapon formed against you will prosper, and every tongue which raises against you in judgment you shall condemn. This is the heritage of the servants of God." It is our heritage to rise above the weapons sent to destroy us. It is wonderful when we discover how the word of God uses eagles to teach us many secrets of life in Christ.

Instead of running from storms like the rest of creation, the eagle flies directly into it allowing the very winds that could destroy it to lift it above the storm. Have you ever been flying when a storm comes and the pilot takes the plane higher above the storm? We need to learn from this example. Jesus is our pilot, and He wants to take us higher so we can not only be closer to Him, but also see things from His perspective. We must allow our pilot Jesus to choose our course, because He alone knows the way of the storm. It is only as we trust Him to choose the course that we are safe from our enemies.

In the other situation where the eagle injured itself by flying into the power lines, we need to realize if we get power from any source other than Jesus, it is destructive. We must keep our eyes on the Son of God.
II Thes. 3:3 states "But the Lord is faithful who will establish you and guard you from the evil one."

When we try to rise above the storms of life on our own, it is like fighting the giants in someone else's armor. We need to face our giants and storms in the power of God's might, not our own. David refused to fight the giant in his life wearing the armor of King Saul that was offered to him. He knew no earthly armor would bring him victory. He had to face his enemy in the name of His God and God himself would defeat the enemy. If you have been fighting the same battle without success, you need to examine your armor and see whose armor you're fighting with. Only the weapons of the Lord will defeat the enemy.

During one of my husband's sermons, he shared an amazing revelation about the armor of God spoken about in Eph. 6:13. This revelation was that we often forget to apply the last part of our armor.

We know to put on the belt of truth, the breastplate of righteousness, and to have our feet fitted with the readiness that comes from the gospel of peace, to take up the shield of faith, put on the helmet of salvation and to use the sword of the Spirit. But we forget the last vital part of our armor, to pray in the spirit. Make sure that you apply the full armor of God daily.

Christians are constantly facing the winds of adversity, but we can use them to enable us to soar higher in Christ. Storms can form strong, godly character if we allow them to. Allow God's power to lift you above the storms of sickness, tragedy, failure and disappointment. Remember, it is not the burdens of life that weigh us down, but how we handle them. Go higher in God so you can look at things from God's view. Your attitude determines your altitude.

I hope by the end of this book you will begin to look at the storms in your life as opportunities to go higher in God where you can get His perspective.

Remember, peace is not present when everything is going well, but is present in the midst of our storms when we focus on God.

Chapter 4

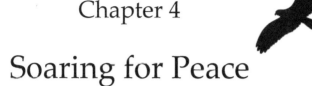

Soaring for Peace

"The LORD gives strength to his people; the LORD blesses his people with peace." PS 29:11 NIV

The Power of the Sun (Son)

There are many times in our life when we encounter attacks from various sources. Some of these attacks are just enough to torment us. The eagle provides an amazing example of what to do when this happens. When the eagle is in lower elevations sometimes smaller birds, like crows, torment the eagle. The crows chase them pulling at their tail feathers and scream to scare off the eagle's prey. It's interesting to me that the tormenters goal is to cut off their food supply. When we don't eat, we become weak physically and spiritually. The enemy of our soul comes to wear us out through the circumstances we encounter daily. He tries to cut off our spiritual food supply. He creates doubt in our minds about the goodness of our God through our daily circumstances. The eagle knows when other birds torment them all they have to do is to fly straight towards the sun.

By God's design, the eagle can fly looking into the sun, but its enemies cannot. Their eyes were not designed to look upon the sun the way the eagles were. So their enemies cannot follow them when they go towards the sun. It is also true of our lives. Our enemies cannot follow us when we fly toward the Son, Jesus Christ.

It is in the heavens, high above the storms and its enemies, that the eagle experiences peace. As we follow the eagle's example and look to the Son, we too will experience peace. Our enemies cannot and will not follow us when we go towards the Son. Jesus conquered all the enemies of our soul on the cross.

One of my favorite quotes is a line from a song performed by Scott Krippane. "Sometimes God calms the storms and sometimes God lets the storm rage on, but He calms His child." This speaks volumes to me about the greatness of God. If God calms the storm then only the storm is changed, but if God calms His child in the midst of the storm, then He has changed His child!

"Peace is not something that can be manufactured. It is divinely and supernaturally given. It is a glorious consequence of God's presence in the soul." (From Everyday Light)

The storm can not penetrate the presence of God. Job 38:1 states, "Then the LORD answered Job out of the storm." This scripture in Job just humbles me to realize that the Lord answered Job out of the storm. God is in your storm and He will answer you if you get your eyes off the storm and onto Him.

PS 68:4 says, "Sing to God, sing praise to his name, extol him who rides on the clouds, his name is the LORD and rejoice before him."

II Thes. 3:16 states, "Now may the God of peace Himself give you peace always in every way." This means, we can have peace in every difficulty.

Recognizing that everything is "Father Filtered" for the children of God, will help us to rise above the storms in our lives. Romans 8:28 teaches us that "all things work together for good to those that love God and are called according to His purpose." To experience peace, we need to look to the God of Peace. We do not experience peace due to our circumstances, but we experience peace *in* our circumstances because, we are children of God who look directly to the Son.

PS 29:11 states, "The LORD gives strength to his people; the LORD blesses his people with peace." The way to have perfect peace is to keep our mind on the Lord. ISA 26:3 says, "You will keep in perfect peace him whose mind is steadfast, because he trusts in you."

In these troubled times we live in, it is very important to realize that God has made a covenant of peace with us. ISA 54:10 states, "Though the mountains be shaken and the hills be removed, yet my unfailing love for you will not be shaken nor my covenant of peace be removed, says the LORD, who has compassion on you."

Wow! What an amazing God we serve. His love is unfailing, and he will never remove His Covenant of Peace.

I want to share with you an amazing journey about this covenant of peace. My father made the decision that I was to go to school in Virginia my senior year. He was sending me there to help my older sister with her children while her husband was in the Navy. I did not want to leave my senior year, but telling my father no was never an option. So as I cried myself to sleep, I prayed that God would change my father's mind. I felt my dad was making a mistake sending me to Virginia, yet the Bible tells me to obey my parents. It does not tell me to obey them only when they are right!

I have made many mistakes in my life, but God gave me the understanding early that if I honor the authority over me then I will be blessed As I was preparing to pack to move to Virginia, I received a phone call from a manager at McDonald's asking me to come in for an interview. My father decided that if I got a job I could stay and finish my senior year at my school.   The phone call came from the man who would become my husband, God's destiny for my life. It has been through the love and encouragement of my husband that I am even writing this book. I believe I had the lowest self esteem of any one I knew, largely in part to the environment I grew up in. But God designed this journey for me to cause me to soar like the eagles above all the difficulties in my life.

God can change any circumstance that is taking you away form His will for your life, if you position yourself to receive His plan. As a child, I did not understand peace because it was not often in our home. So my entire life has been a journey of discovering peace. I am learning that peace is not obtained in the absence of trouble or storms but in the midst of them. I always looked at other people's lives and wondered why they experienced peace and I didn't. It was because I did not understand this Covenant of Peace.

Chapter Five

Soaring for Perspective

"If people can't see what God is doing, they stumble all over themselves. But when they attend to what God reveals they are blessed." Proverbs 29:18 (The Message Bible)

Eagles have tremendous vision. Their ability to focus on far away things is eight times stronger than the human eye. They can spot a rabbit two miles away! At half a mile they can see scales on a fish. But it is only when an eagle soars that it gets a full perspective. This is true of us as Christians. The higher you go in God the greater your perspective. Your perspective will only be as high as you are. Can you imagine how God's perspective is?

He created everything and knows the beginning from the end!

Proverbs 29:18 (The Message Bible) states "If people can't see what God is doing, they stumble all over themselves. But when they attend to what God reveals they are blessed."

Remember, it is not the burdens of life that weigh us down, but how we handle them. Your attitude determines your altitude. When we have the proper perspective then we realize we cannot choose how others will treat us, but we can choose how we will respond to how we have been treated. *Our reaction is our choice.* I am beginning to understand that when you walk with Christ, rejection is just direction. We need to submit our lives into His hands and trust Him completely. It was rejection that prepared the way of the cross for Christ. You must rise above the storm in order to get the proper perspective. Not getting the right perspective in a storm can cause you to be driven off course. This takes us away from the purpose the storm was sent to accomplish. I have not had the correct perspective of who I am.

I wanted to go to college but was not given the opportunity due to finances. When I got married, I was quite fulfilled being a wife and eventually a mother of two boys. But in the back of my mind I always felt I could never have a career. My need for a career would become the reason for many storms ahead. My grandmother told me I would not succeed in life and I believed her. It was this belief that allowed me to be treated very cruel, in the workplace. Being out of the will of God will always cause pain. I did not believe in whom I was or what I could accomplish, and those lies of my childhood would surface anytime I began to attempt flight.

The enemy of our soul will always bring the things of our past up to keep us from reaching the place of true perspective. You see the devil is not all knowing like God, so he is limited to using our past against us. We must remember the place of agreement is the place of power. We must align ourselves with what the Bible says about us. We should never listen to any source that is contrary to the word of God.

My greatest area of defeat has always been in the area of finances. We have had so many financial struggles in our lives. I went through a season when I felt like God needed my help to provide for us. Even though God had given me a wonderful husband who always used the principles in the word of God about finances, I was never satisfied. Some of the storms we encounter are of our own making, just like Jonah when he disobeyed God.

Regardless of where the storm originates, God has purpose in it. We only need to surrender our will for His. We always tithed and were givers, but my husband was working in Christian television before going into fulltime ministry. His paychecks would sometimes be two to three weeks late because the money was just not there to meet payroll. Because I did not have the correct perspective about God's provision in my life, I developed mistrust in God. This caused my husband to feel like I did not trust him either. We now offer marriage counseling from the lessons that those turbulent storms produced.

God wants you to know if you are His child, He is in your boat, and that the winds and waves obey Him. We must remember God used a great storm to rescue Jonah from going his own way. What Jonah experienced in the storm was better than what he would have experienced if he had continued to go away from God.

Think of it! The storm was sent to save him from himself. I have finally surrendered my will for His will. I may never have a career, but I know that I will succeed at what God has called me to, not because of me or anything I do, but because I am His and He will accomplish it through me. God requires us to be faithful, not successful. If we remain faithful, we will be successful!

You see my life's journey was never meant to be about me, but about what God can accomplish in and through me. I would not be writing this book if it had not been for the storms in my life. Some of them have been at my own doing. Others have been sent to rescue me, and some have been from the enemy.

Regardless of where the storms originated, if we are children of God then He will work all things for good in our lives as we surrender to Him. Be a spiritual storm chaser! Face your storms with confidence in God and let them be avenues of insight and change in your life.

Chapter Six

Soaring for Pleasure

"Let them shout for joy and be glad, Who favor my righteous cause; And let them say continually, "Let the Lord be magnified, Who has pleasure in the prosperity of His servant." Psalms 35:27 NKJV

The study of eagles reveals that eagles sometimes soar just for the fun of it. We need to learn from the eagles. We need to enjoy life. The eagle's relationship with its mate is strengthened by soaring together for fun. In the marriage relationship too often the conflicts and busy schedules keep us from soaring together and enjoying each other's company.

I enjoy my husband's company. The quantity of time you spend in any relationship will determine the quality of that relationship. The more time you spend with God the closer you will be with Him. This is true of any relationship. It's hard to enjoy life when you are constantly worried about everything you do or don't do.

I was so broken that I always questioned everything I did. Worry invaded my life on a daily basis. I'm sure I was not enjoyable to be around. I would always take the road that lead to negative thinking. You can never soar for pleasure when you worry about everything in life. God tells us to give no thought of tomorrow. His grace is sufficient for us each day.

I was given a prophecy once that I almost missed the things of God because I was always living for tomorrow. Live each day God has given you to its fullest. How gracious, patient and understanding God and my husband were with me during these times. Worry was a generational curse I needed to take authority over. I am now on the road that uses faith instead of fear. It takes the same effort to have fear or faith. It all depends on where your focus is. In every situation of our lives we get to choose which road we take, either faith or fear.

The interest I have in eagles began when my husband and I took a trip from Greensburg, PA, to the Grand Canyon on our motorcycle. It was on this trip that I saw my first eagle in the wild. The whole miracle of our trip was part of the journey I would take to learn how to soar. When Dale and I first began our journey together, he told me about a dream he had. He desired to go to the Grand Canyon on a motorcycle for our 25th Wedding Anniversary. We were not even married yet when he told me about his dream. How amazing that he had vision for our future. As married couples you need to dream together. We have not been taught the importance of vision.

Dale only mentioned his dream to me and a few family members over the next twenty-four years. But God knew his dream and reminded his brother, Duane, about it. On our 24th wedding anniversary, Duane called and said that God reminded him of Dale's dream. He told Dale to come to West Virginia and get his motorcycle. We only had one year to prepare for the trip. I had never ridden before and was not sure I could do it, but I always want to be a part of making my husband's dreams come true. I believed that if

God provided the motorcycle, then He would work out all the other details. I was not used to doing anything just for the pleasure of it. I would always count the cost and say we couldn't afford whatever it was.

God wants us to enjoy the life He gave us. We need to have times that we soar just for pleasure. This is one of the things I learned on our trip. We traveled 7200 miles getting there and back. It was the best time of my life. God taught me to depend on Him in ways I had never experienced before.

Whenever you prefer your mate and are a part of fulfilling their dreams, then you are the one who is blessed. My husband loves golf. The few times I have gone golfing I did not enjoy it. However, on my husband's 50th birthday I wanted to give him a special gift. I saved my money and got a husband and wife membership at a local golf course. I now go with him and love it. I am the one who received the blessing by preferring my husband. I am not the best golfer, but the time I spend with him is priceless. He is God's special gift to me. I enjoy spending time with him over anyone else. I am able to declare this now because I found the purpose in the storms we had to endure in our marriage.

Sometimes in life it is the roughest roads that take us to the most beautiful places. I have a great marriage and it's not because we've had all easy sailing, but rather that we have faced the storms and grown stronger because of them. We need to learn from the eagle that life was meant to be enjoyed. We should strive to develop an attitude of thanksgiving for the things God has given us. He has given each of us all the ability to soar above our circumstances if we wait on Him. We should choose to soar, not just to overcome our troubles, but in the good times as well. We should soar just for the pleasure of it. We need to look to God in everything so we can enjoy the journey.

It is in rising higher that we get a heavenly view and discover God's fingerprints on the things we encounter. Just like the eagle, we were created to soar. This is how we discover our full potential in God and find our destiny.

The eagle has a wingspan of 7 to 8 feet. It can reach an altitude of 12,000 feet in just minutes. Airline pilots regularly see eagles soaring high above the earth at heights other birds can not achieve. An eagle can reach 25,000 feet, which is 5 miles above the earth. They soar so high that ice sometimes forms on their wings.

We were created to soar, and when we do, we discover the joy is in the journey. Many times we focus so much on where we want to be, we forget to enjoy where we are. Nehemiah 8:10b tells us that the joy of the Lord is our strength. If you want to have strength in your journey then your joy needs to be in the Lord, not in your circumstances.

Chapter 7

Soaring for Purity

"He who loves purity of heart and has grace on his lips, the king will be his friend." Proverbs 22:11 NKJV

Sometimes eagles get a buildup on their beaks, caused by a small virus. This virus causes the eagle to be off balance so it can't land properly. It is very important in our Christian walk that we stay balanced. Proverbs 11:1 tells us *"a false balance is an abomination to the Lord: but a just weight is His delight."* The eagle knows it has to get rid of the virus, so with its God-given instinct it soars up into the heavens so high that the altitude kills the virus! Do you see how important purity can be in our lives?

When the eagle is free from the virus it can fly again unhindered. Most of the things in our lives that keep us from being balanced can only be broken off when we go higher in God. Think just for a minute about what you have allowed to buildup in your life that is hindering your walk with God. What has caused you to be off balance? Hidden sins, unforgiveness, resentment (these are just to name a few.) Allow the wind of the Holy Spirit to lift you into the presence of God where these things can be broken off.

In my life, the thing that always kept me off balance was worry. Worry means "to divide into parts." It caused me to be preoccupied with things like stress, anxiety and fear. Jesus speaks against worry in Matthew 6:25 and 26. "Therefore I say to you 'do not worry' about your life, what you will eat or drink, nor about your body, what you will put on. Look at the birds of the air, for they neither sow or reap nor gather into barns: yet your heavenly Father feeds them. Are you not of more value than they?"

God revealed to me that I had trouble trusting Him because I did not believe that I was valuable. My whole childhood I was made to feel like I had no value. Rejection was a faithful friend. I needed a revelation of my worth! Even though my wonderful husband and the scriptures told me that I was a person of worth, I could not receive it because I had not forgiven my grandmother for always making me feel invaluable. Just like the eagle I had allowed something to attach its self to me. In order to brake off the hold it had on me I had to go higher in God and receive His help to forgive. Forgiveness is just a choice! I had to choose to forgive, but the hurt went so deep in my heart I could not even forgive without the help of my heavenly Father. I prayed and asked God to forgive her and everyone else who had constantly rejected me. It was then that I discovered that when you are a Christian seeking the will of God in your life, then rejection is just direction.

Remember I said earlier, the place of agreement is the place of power? Be very careful who and what you agree with. When I positioned myself to agree with other's words about me instead of what God said about me, it gave the enemy a legal right to stay in my life and constantly use circumstances to align me to the wrong way of thinking.

This is a lesson I needed to learn before I could began to fulfill my destiny as a pastor's wife. Being in the ministry is not an easy place. You will always have someone coming against you when you are trying to minister.
I needed to learn to align myself up with the word of God or I would never be able to minister. God in His loving kindness and mercy did not lead my husband into the ministry until later in life. God knows the brokenness I've had in my life. He waited until I was able to forgive. And the thing that was my greatest weakness has become the arena that I minister from. What a loving heavenly Father we have!

Eagles know the importance of purification so much that they often stir up their nest. The nest can become messy and cluttered with debris. Old fish rotting, and infested with maggots accumulate in the nest, so the eagle is always cleaning house. This is a very important lesson for us! What we allow in our homes, and our hearts, will also come out of our homes and our hearts. My husband offers a devotional teaching to the men in our church where he emphasizes the importance of purity. One of the things he teaches them is sexual purity. He shows them the importance of covenant and they are given the opportunity to sign an agreement of sexual purity with their wife. Dale carries his agreement in his Bible. He brought it to me one day and asked me to sign it with him. It states that with the help of Almighty God, he will endeavor to set no evil thing before his eyes. Rejoice with the wife of his youth and put on the whole armor of God. *Purity is so important.*
Proverbs 20:11 states, "Even a child is known by his actions, by whether his conduct is pure and right."

Matthew 5:8 says, "Blessed are the pure in heart, for they will see God".
Matthew 10:26 states, "that there is nothing covered, that shall not be made known. "

I have lived my life on the principle that if I judge myself then I will not be judged. If we reveal the hidden things, they cannot be used as tools of the enemy to destroy us. If we refuse to reveal them the enemy will allow them to remain hidden until the revelation of them destroys the most people. We have seen this in many fallen ministries.

You need to reveal the hidden things of your life to God so he can forgive, cleanse and restore you. When you reveal the hidden things to God, His grace is there to heal and restore. God is a great God. Nothing is impossible for Him. God has promised to work all things out for our good when we place them in His hands. The key is to place them into His hands and not to keep them hidden in our hearts. Check your life by stirring up your nest for purification. Proverbs 16:6 of the Message Bible says that "guilt is banished through love and truth." My desire for you is that you will not only see the importance of purity, but you will follow the eagle's example and continually stir up your heart to see what shouldn't be there.

Chapter Eight

Vision

"Where there is no vision, the people are unrestrained, but happy is he who keeps the law." Proverbs 29:18 New American Standard

The eagle has amazing vision. They can see what other birds cannot. It has always been my desire to see what others cannot. I desire to have eyes of compassion and to see things in the light of their eternal worth. The journey is always easier when you know where you are going. This was one of the lessons I learned when we took three weeks off work to go to the Grand Canyon on our motorcycle for our 25th wedding anniversary. Due to the time it took to get there and back we did not have much time to site see. We were just outside of Bryce Canyon at Escalante National Park. Dale asked the park ranger what would be the best thing to see in the park. We were told there was an incredible waterfall most people don't get to see because it required a three mile walk through a box canyon. We decided to hike through the desert to the waterfall.

I will never forget the spiritual lessons I learned from this journey. First, I learned you need to be prepared. The preparation needed for this trip was water, good walking shoes, a hiking stick and more water. We learned very quickly the desert sun has a way of drying you out. We were not as prepared for the journey as we should have been.

In our Christian walk we need to be prepared for the spiritual journey. We must make sure our feet are firmly secure in our rock Jesus. We need to be led by the Son of God. We need to stay on the path He has chosen for us, to protect us from the serpent, and we need the water of the word.

Dale and I started on our three mile hike with only one bottle of water to share. Not having enough water made the journey harder. We knew the hike was about three miles one way, but because we had never been there, we weren't sure of the distance or the surroundings. We kept passing what we thought were mile markers. We later found out that they were just points of interest. At one point I felt the journey was too long and difficult so we almost turned back. Don't ever stop short of your destination. Dale has often reminded our church that when you are digging yourself out of a cave the darkness looks the same whether you are six feet or six inches away from freedom. Don't let your surroundings dictate your reaction. Never give up!

We passed others on the trail that had already reached the waterfall and were on their way back. We asked them how much farther we had to go and if the journey was worth it? Everyone said the journey was worth it, even though the path was long and very difficult. I not only doubted my ability to reach our destination but also my ability to return before night fall. It would have been very dangerous to travel at night in the box canyon. There were signs with warnings not to venture off the trail. The encouragement of others kept us going. It is very important in the life of a Christian to give and receive encouragement. Finally, we reached our destination. As we approached the waterfall the temperature dropped several degrees and there was a refreshing wind blowing. The waterfall was surrounded by trees. It is impossible to describe the beauty of what we saw. I have never seen water as clear as that coming off the rocks of the falls.

God taught me so many valuable lessons through this adventure. As Christians, the joy is in the journey and the destination is worth it! All the trials and difficulties we must endure to reach our destination are worth it. Hebrews 12:2 states: "Looking unto Jesus the author and finisher of our faith, who for the joy that was set before him endured the cross, despising the shame, and is set down at the right hand of the throne of God."
This same scripture in the Message Bible reads "keep your eyes on Jesus, who both began and finished this race we're in. Study how he did it. Because he never lost sight of where he was headed, that exhilarating finish in and with God, he could put up with anything along the way; cross, shame, whatever. And now He's there, in the place of honor, right alongside God. Just think, for the joy that was set before Christ, He endured the cross. You and I were that joy! Jesus would rather die than live without you!

There were several times we almost turned back when the journey was too difficult because we weren't sure where we were going. The way back was just as long, just as hot and just as grueling, but we knew our destination and that made the trip much easier. We can have confidence in God to see us through any situation. God loves us too much to force His will on us, so He just waits for us to relinquish control.

God knows our hearts so we can't fool Him. He will reward those who diligently seek Him. We need to seek

His ways not ours! We need to get a revelation of the love God has for us. How can we doubt God's goodness towards us when He sent His only Son to die in our place? When you are going through a storm and can't see what's going on, trust that God's heart for you is only good.

Do you know God in an advisory capacity, or do you know Him as a loving Father, whose heart is always only good towards His child? The answer to this question will help you determine how high in God you are. Some Christians never rise above the storm because they don't realize the storm has purpose.

I now know God is good, and I can lovingly refer to him as "daddy" God. What a difference! I went from blaming God for all the wrong in my life to trusting Him. What a freedom this offers when you see God for who He is and not just for what He does.

I pray you will have a renewed vision for your life, the vision given by God that will truly bring you freedom.

Chapter Nine

Commitment

"Pay attention, come close now, listen carefully to my life-giving, life-nourishing words. I'm making a lasting covenant commitment with you, the same I made with David: sure, solid, enduring love." Isaiah 55: 3 (The Message Bible)

One of the things that distinguish an eagle is commitment. The eagle mates for life! They are committed to their mates and their family. If someone was asked to describe you, would they describe you as a person of commitment? Are you a person that keeps your word? Are you trustworthy? Do you keep covenant?

Deut. 7:9 says, "Therefore know that the Lord your God He is God, the faithful God who keeps covenant and mercy to a thousand generations with those who love Him and keep His commandments."

Our attitude to our mates is governed by our attitude towards God. Love alone is not enough to hold a marriage together; it takes commitment and knowing the power of Covenant. When two Christians marry, God stands as a witness to the marriage, sealing it with covenant. The power of a covenant keeping God stands behind a husband and wife who live according to their marriage vows. What a blessing to know that God backs up our marriage with His power and authority to stand against every enemy that would threaten it from without or within.

Eagles mate for life. They do not flock together like other birds. Once an eagle chooses a mate, he will stay with her for life. They live an average of 30 to 50 years and will stay together until one of the partners dies. No matter what happens, the marriage will last until one of the eagles dies. Eagles also guard their marriage by watching for infiltrators. This is a lesson we should learn to guard our marriage relationships. I can walk into a room full of women I have never met, and know almost instantly which ones are looking for a relationship at any cost. These are the ones who would pursue a married man. I pray for Dale, and I honor and respect him. He is my gift from God, and we are one.

Work on things together. Dream together. Always remember, there isn't a storm that you can't rise above when you allow the wind of God's spirit to lift you. You must continually invest in your mate because sooner or later you will make a withdrawal, and you must be careful to invest more than you withdraw.

Eagles carry out the most incredible courtship, one that continues throughout their lives together. During the mating season, a spectacular midair ceremony will take place. A female will carry a stick high into the air and drop it near a prospective male. If he is interested, he will respond to her by swooping down to catch the stick and return it to her. This dropping and retrieving of the stick may be repeated many times. To complete their mating ceremony, both eagles will soar to a great height, lock talons together, and freefall towards the earth together. The female will not try to break their freefall to earth until the male releases his powerful grip. What an example of trust!

Their love songs have been heard by observers of this amazing display. This ritual is a vow of complete and total trust. Many species of eagles will perform this ceremony again throughout their lives as a sign of devotion. They also show affection the way they gently groom and stroke each other. Take the example from the eagle and continue to date after you are married. Enjoy one another's company! This takes work. But you can never receive from a place you have not invested. Invest in each other. The male eagle continues to court his mate the rest of her life. Don't neglect each other. Spend time with, and enjoy the gift God has given you in each other. Proverbs 18: 22 says, "He who finds a wife finds a good thing and obtains favor from the Lord."

Eagles are also very defensive of their young. They will attack anything that poses a threat. We need to guard our homes and children. What we do as parents speaks louder than what we say. Lead your children by example. One of the greatest honors we have had was when our son Jason shared at our 25th wedding anniversary. He said that he and Kim have a good marriage because of the example Dale and I have shown in our marriage. Jon wrote us the most wonderful thank you after he graduated from Christ for the Nations Bible College. Our marriage has not been perfect, but our children have seen the power of our love and commitment to Christ, and to each other. Children learn what you model for them.

Chapter Ten

Leading by Example

*"And it wasn't because we didn't have a right to your
support; we did. We simply wanted to provide an example of
diligence, hoping it would prove contagious."*
(The Message Bible)

Everything Jesus taught He lived.

I Peter 5:8 remind us to *"be sober, be vigilant: because your
adversary the devil, as a roaring lion walks about seeking whom
he may devour."* One thing God showed me about this
scripture is that you can always hear a roaring lion's
approach. We need to look and listen for anything that
would threaten the safety of our home. Think about your
home. What would you get rid of if you knew Jesus was
coming for a visit?

Dale and I would guard what our children watched on
television. We would anoint our house with oil and pray
for God's peace to be in our home. My husband and I
would guard the unity in our home. Once, when he was
preaching he told a true story about how lions hunt. When
a lion becomes too old to hunt, he just stays in one place
and roars; his prey will always run away from the sound
of the roaring lion, right into the path of the younger lions
that are waiting in the opposite direction. Always seek
God about the direction you should go. Psalms 133: 1-3
tells us that *"where there is unity God commands a blessing."*

Proverbs 10:22 says, *"the blessing of the Lord makes one rich and He adds no sorrow with it."* So one of the keys to being rich and obtaining the blessing of the Lord is to walk in unity. Make your homes a place of unity! You can not have unity if you are always looking out for your own interests and desires. James 3:16 states that *"where envy and self-seeking exist, confusion and every evil thing is there."* This is a strong warning to us! Just think every evil work. We need to learn the importance of unity. Confusion is not of God. I Cor. 14:33 tells us that God is not the author of confusion, so any time there is confusion, we know it is not of God. Isaiah 61:7 tells us that *"instead of your shame you shall have double honor. And instead of confusion you shall rejoice in a double portion."*

Eagles make great parents. Once the eggs are laid, the eagles settle down to a pretty quiet life. Our lives are so busy that we often see our children as hindrances instead of blessings. Psalms 127:3 of The Message says, "Don't you see that children are God's best gift?"

As I was praying one day, I realized that the best I had to offer God was my boys. So I have given them back to God, with a confidence that He will keep them. My desire has always been that they will spend their lives for God, because I know that the only thing we can take to heaven with us is other people. Everything else in this life will come to an end. My prayer for you is that you will not waste your life on things that don't matter in eternity. We live in a society that keeps us so busy we forget to enjoy the journey. We should spend our lives on things that will outlast us. We need to be more concerned about succeeding at something that doesn't matter, than being concerned about our failures.

I love the teaching John Maxwell gives on the difference between leaving an inheritance or a legacy.

"Inheritance is something you give to others that temporarily brings happiness. It eventually fades as it is spent and your activity may or may not pay off. A legacy is something you place in others that permanently transforms them. It lives on long after you are gone and your activity becomes achievement. "

The eagle parents leave a legacy not only to their eaglets, but also to us. If we model their example about the storms we face, then we will be permanently transformed. The female eagle devotes herself to guarding the eggs and keeping them warm. The male brings food, and for brief periods each day, he relieves her of her duty. When the eaglets are born the male is busy; he hunts food from dawn to dusk. The male takes turns watching the eaglets, and if the female dies he will raise the young alone. What dedication!

They also provide constant protection to their young. The eagles use their wings to protect their young from the storms, from the heat and cold, and to hide them from their enemies. In Psalms 36:7 we read, "How precious is thy loving kindness O God. Therefore the children of men put their trust under the shadow of your wings." Psalms 61:4 says, "I will abide in thy tabernacle forever, I will trust in the cover of thy wings." Psalms 57:1b states, "in the shadow of thy wings I will make my refuge, until my calamities are past."

Position yourself to receive the constant protection of your Heavenly Father by invitation. Invite Him into all the areas of your life. He is waiting for you!

Chapter Eleven

Knowing the Seasons

"To everything there is a season and a time to every purpose under the heaven." Ecclesiastes 3:1 NKJV

When we get an understanding of this scripture it will help us to weather any storm. We will realize no matter how difficult a season we are in, that it will eventually change. You can make it through anything when you have hope.

I always knew truth had a voice because the Bible tells us that the truth will set us free, but I never knew hope had a door. God showed me in Hosea 2:15 that He offers a door of hope to us. *"Therefore, behold I will allure her. I will bring her into the wilderness and speak comfort to her. I will give her vineyards from there and the Valley of Achor as a door of hope: She will sing there as in the days of her youth, as in the day when she came up from the land of Egypt."* When you read this in The Spirit Filled Bible it shows us that the wilderness here is not a place of punishment, but a place of privacy.

When you pull yourself away into a place of privacy with God, He will open the door of hope for you. "Achor" means trouble, and was the scene of Achen's sin in Joshua 7:26. God redeems situations, bringing present hope in the place of previous trouble. I love this! It would be great to have God open a door of hope, but when He takes us to a place of previous trouble and redeems it, this shows an even greater revelation of His redeeming power. Oh, if we would only meet God in the wilderness to find the redemption we need in our current places of trouble. He invites you now! Surrender to Him!

Keep reminding yourself that seasons change. It will give you the ability to look forward to the good days that are ahead. Change is never easy but is necessary. The eagle is the greatest example to us of this.

When it is time for the eaglets to leave the nest, the mother eagle begins removing anything that is comfortable. God, in his infinite wisdom, uses the one who made the nest so comfortable, as the one who removes the comfort. The mother eagle will pluck feathers from her own body to line the nest with feathers before the eaglets are born. However, when it is time for them to fly, she will remove anything that will keep them in their comfort zone. God does the same thing with His children. Amos 6:1 warns, "Woe to them that are at ease in Zion." Zion means, "a parched place. " If you are comfortable being in a dry place, you need to experience a fresh move of God. Comfort zones are the place where most people live. It is the place where we easily lose interest and we are hard to motivate. This is also a place where opposition is weak and mistakes are very costly. Victories are never achieved by staying in your comfort zone.

Below is a list of what causes people to remain in their comfort zones:

1. A lack of hunger and thirst.
2. An unwillingness to sacrifice.
3. Never wanting to address personal issues or failures.
4. Living in our yesterdays.
5. Being physically, emotionally or spiritually tired.
6. being unwilling to change.
7. Staying busy doing small things.
8. Allowing bad experiences to keeping us from trying.

How to overcome our comfort zones:

1. John Bevere says, we hunger for what we feed on, so Begin feeding on the word of God.
2. Be willing to sacrifice.
3. Invite the Holy Spirit into your personal issues and failures.
4. Live for the day you are in because the things of God are made up of what everyday brings.
5. Seek help for your physical, emotional and spiritual needs.
6. Be willing to change.
7. Busy yourself for the things that will last.
8. Allow your bad experiences to be a launching board to move forward.

Louis Pasteur continued to work on vaccines during the month his three daughters died of the disease he was trying to prevent. He used his failures as a launching board to succeed.

John Milton continued to write poetry although he was

blind, and Beethoven composed music even though he was deaf. These are examples of what can be accomplished when we refuse to stay in our comfort zones.

The mother eagle knows the eaglet will never reach the heights it was intended for by staying in the nest. So, out of love for her offspring, she will remove everything that would keep them from flying. This speaks so loudly to me because it was very difficult to give my boys wings.

My husband and I moved to pastor a church. When we moved, our oldest son had just married and our youngest son went to Youth with a Mission for school. So for the first time, I was not taking care of our children. Not only were we in a new place where we only knew the Pastor who had hired us, but we were going there with empty nest syndrome. This was a very big season of change for me. I will never forget the void I felt when the boys left home. But God, and my wonderful husband, ministered to me in this season of change. When we left our home in West Virginia, our oldest son Jason, and his new wife Kim, moved into our home there. Our youngest son, Jon, left for Montana on a three-day train ride. Jon was going to Missions school to go to Nepal and India. This was definitely giving our boys wings. You cannot impact the world for Christ, if you never leave the nest.

Our children are our best gifts from God and the best gifts we could give back to God. After several years of marriage our boys have given us four grandchildren. Jason and Kim have a daughter, Zoe. Jon and Aimee have two girls, Alivia and Emberly and a son, Levi.

Empty nest syndrome was not an easy transition for me. When I let go, and was willing to trust God, the beauty that came is hard to describe. We began opening our home to international students, and we now have several spiritual children all over the world. One of the students that lived with us now lives in Beijing and still calls us Mom and Dad. His name is Jianbin and he now has a beautiful wife named Qing. They are true blessings in our lives. We also have a wonderful Chinese daughter named Ping, a son-in-law named Bill, and a grandson named Andrew, from our empty nest years. God used the changing of the seasons to enlarge our home, and our hearts. We have several spiritual children in Peru from our mission trips there. Patty, Millie, Gabby, Teddy, Anita, Saulo, Christina, William and Ruth are a result of the changing seasons in our life. These people have enriched our lives in so many ways. You cannot, and will not, accomplish your destiny unless you embrace the changes in your life. One way you can determine whether or not you have embraced change is to examine your thought life. Do you spend most of your time thinking about the past, the present or the future? If you are thinking mostly about the past, or the future, then you have not embraced change. You can not experience victory today living in your yesterdays. The things of God are made up of what each day brings. The Bible tells us to give no thought about tomorrow.

The eagle knows how important it is to discern the times and the seasons. When it is time for the eaglets to fly, the parents will withhold food to create a deep hunger in them. The mother then circles the nest, holds food in one talon and calls out to them. The eaglet tries to snatch the food, nearing the edge of the nest. All of a sudden the young bird loses its balance and topples out of the nest. Both the parents will fly to the young birds rescue, screaming encouragement and instruction. If the eaglet continues to struggle, one of the parents will fly close and create a change in the air current providing an updraft to lift the eaglet.

The Holy Spirit is our helper, and will come along side of us with the wind of the Spirit to cause an updraft to lift us up. The Holy Spirit is the wind beneath our wings. In Exodus 19:4 it says "I bore you on eagle's wings"

In Hebrew, the word "bore" means to raise, to lift up, and to help. Look to the Holy Spirit when you need assistance flying.

God invites and leads us out of our comfort zones to explore the heights for which we were designed. He creates a hunger in us for the perfect will of God. When we were in Bryce Canyon on our motorcycle trip, I saw a beautiful picture of a mountain goat leaping over a large crevice. The caption on the picture simply said "Faith"! I loved this picture so much, Dale bought it for me and had it shipped home. One day when I was dusting it I told God that I wanted faith like that; then I realized the mountain goat was only doing what it was created to do. We have been created to soar! Spread your spiritual wings and allow the wind of the Spirit to lift you up where you belong, high above the storms in your life.

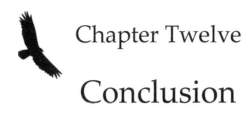 Chapter Twelve

Conclusion

"But those who hope in the Lord shall renew their strength; they will soar on wings like eagles." Isaiah 40: 31 NIV

It is my desire that you experience the renewed strength the Bible teaches in Isaiah 40:31; that as you hope in the Lord your strength will be renewed. That you will soar on wings like the eagle, and that you will see the storms in your life as opportunities to go higher in God.

I pray you will follow the eagle's example and soar for peace, perspective, pleasure and purity. Always teach by your example of patience and commitment.

I would like to end this book with the following letter that was sent to me via email from: emailministry@emailministry.org.

"When you thought I wasn't looking," by a child.

This is a message every parent should read, because your children are watching and doing as you do, not as you say.

When you thought I wasn't looking I saw you hang my first painting on the refrigerator, and I immediately wanted to paint another one.

When you thought I wasn't looking, I saw you feed a stray

cat, and I learned that it was good to be kind to animals.

When you thought I wasn't looking, I saw you make my favorite cake for me and I learned that little things can be the special things in life.

When you thought I wasn't looking, I heard you say a prayer, and I knew there was a God I could always talk to and I learned to trust in God.

When you thought I wasn't looking, I saw you make a meal and take it to a friend who was sick, and I learned that we all have to help take care of each other.

When you thought I wasn't looking, I saw you give of your time and money to help people who had nothing and I learned that those who have something should give to those who don't.

When you thought I wasn't looking, I felt you kiss me goodnight and I felt loved and safe.

When you thought I wasn't looking, I saw you take care of our house and everyone in it and I learned we have to take care of what we have been given.

When you thought I wasn't looking, I say how you handled your responsibilities, even when you didn't feel good and I learned that I had to be responsible when I grew up.

When you thought I wasn't looking, I saw tears come from your eyes and I learned that sometimes things hurt, but it's alright to cry.

When you thought I wasn't looking, I saw that you cared and I wanted to be everything I could be.

When you thought I wasn't looking, I learned most of life's lessons that I need to know to be a good and productive person when I grow up.

When you thought I wasn't looking, I looked at you and wanted to say, thanks for all the things I saw when you thought I wasn't looking.

Author Unknown

We have been given many biblical truths from the eagle when they didn't know we were watching. Take an inventory of your life in the light that someone is watching what you do. Line your life up with the word of God and know that He is in all your storms. Position yourself to allow the storms in your life to be an example to all the people that you may not know are watching. And enjoy your life's story always knowing that God is the author and finisher of your faith and that He who has begun a good work in you will complete it.

Stop and smell the roses along the way. Life is meant to be enjoyed. If you are in a difficult season, know that this season will change. If you are in a storm, know that God is in your boat. Live your life knowing you are of great worth and value; so much so, that Christ died to give you life.... so enjoy your journey.

Epilogue:

I always tell God I am not qualified to do many of the things He has asked me to do. But God always reminds me, when I am weak, He is strong. If I were qualified, I would not rely on God the way I do. So not being qualified, actually qualifies me. This way, God gets all the glory for anything I do, because it is not me, but Christ in me that can do what He has asked of me! I tell people all the time I am God's poster child to show if He can use me, He can use anyone. Don't ever let your inability keep you from the things of God.

As of the publishing of this book, I am facing the greatest storm of my life. However, as I follow the example of the eagle, I will not only rise above it, but by the wind of the Spirit of God I will soar.

BIBLIOGRAPHY

Bevere, John. Drawing Near. Palmer Lake:
    Messenger, 2004.

Carman. Revival in the Land.

Father's Love Letter. May 1999. Father Heart
Communications. 10 May 2010
<http://www.fathersloveletter.con/about.html>.

Greiner, Rev. William Claire. Family Christian Inspiration.
9 Mar. 2004. 24 May 2004
<http://www.famci.com/sermons/eagles.htm>.

Havner, Vance. Quotiki. 2009. 24 May 2004
    <http://www.quotiki.com/quotes/288>.

Hughes, Selwyn. Everyday Light. Nashville: Broadman &
    Holman, 1997.

Jeremiah, David. crosswalk.com. 2002. 25 Feb. 2010
<http://www.crosswalk.com/faith/ministry_articles/1221517>.

Krippane, Scott. Sometimes He Calms the Child.

Livengood, Pati. Photography by Pati. 2011. Pati

        Livengood, Harrison City, PA.

        <www.photographybypati.com>

Maxwell, John. The 21 Irrefutable Laws of Leadership.
    Nashville: Thomas Nelson, 1998.

Rueben, Morgan. On Eagle's Wings.

Simpson, Kevin. <u>Wildlife</u>. 2009. Kevin Simpson, Ruffsdale, PA.
    <www.pbase.con/kdsphotography>.

Stone, Robert C. <u>Eagle Flight</u>. 2006. 16 Sept. 2008

    < http: //www.eagleflight.org/index.html.>.

Wagner, Holly. <u>When It Pours, He Reigns</u>. Nashville:
    Thomas Nelson, 2004.

Into the Storm

You can order "Into the Storm" by going to lulu.com.

It is available as print or as a download.